The
Secret
Me

~ a questionnaire journal ~
VOLUME TWO

Created by:
Shane Windham

NOT INTENDED
FOR USE
BY CHILDREN

At Random

This journal is the property of:

_____

Date begun:

_____

How do you think you will die?

_____

Where would you like to be laid to rest?

_____

Can you write in cursive?
[   ]yes [   ]no
Have you viewed the moon through a telescope?
[   ]yes [   ]no

What is the most unhealthy food one can consume?

_____

Do you recycle?
[   ]yes [   ]no

How many planets in the universe are home to intelligent life?

_____

What do you think would most likely spark a third world war?

_____

Should Pluto be considered a planet?
[   ]yes [   ]no
Do you have more than one source of income?
[   ]yes [   ]no

At Random

Do you usually remove the tags from your clothing?
[   ]yes [   ]no

Did your parents care if you swore around them?
[   ]yes [   ]no

Would you consider yourself part of a large family?
[   ]yes [   ]no

Do you save the various greeting cards people give you?
[   ]yes [   ]no

Have you had a seizure?
[   ]yes [   ]no

Where do you like to sit when watching a movie in a theater?

_____

Do you usually make it a point to carry cash on you?
[   ]yes [   ]no

Do you associate with coworkers outside of the workplace?
[   ]yes [   ]no

Do you enjoy speaking to an audience?
[   ]yes [   ]no

Why did the chicken cross the road?

_____

Would you be interested in bird watching as a hobby?
[   ]yes [   ]no

Have you been diagnosed with scoliosis?
[   ]yes [   ]no

Do you usually sleep with a fan on?
[   ]yes [   ]no

Would you want to live through a disfiguring fire?
[   ]yes [   ]no

Do you like wearing watches?
[   ]yes [   ]no

RECOMMENDED: *The Secret Me: A Questionnaire Journal*

At Random

Have you been on a double date?

[   ]yes [   ]no

Do you know how to properly eat food with chopsticks?

[   ]yes [   ]no

What, instead of money, should we offer homeless people?

_____

Have you rented a vehicle?

[   ]yes [   ]no

Have you participated in a marketing survey?

[   ]yes [   ]no

Do you normally finish one book before beginning another?

[   ]yes [   ]no

Do you currently have a life insurance policy?

[   ]yes [   ]no

Have you purchased an infomercial product?

[   ]yes [   ]no

Do you have a resume?

[   ]yes [   ]no

Have you fallen while walking down a flight of stairs?

[   ]yes [   ]no

Have you wished someone a happy birthday
when it wasn't their birthday?

[   ]yes [   ]no

Which of the original seven world wonders would you most like to see?

_____

Do you think there's likely some type of life in Europa's oceans?

[   ]yes [   ]no

Do you own a gun?

[   ]yes [   ]no

RECOMMENDED: *The Secret Me: A Questionnaire Journal*

Multiple Choice

Which of the following interests you most?
___Lateral thinking puzzles   ___Mental math problems
___Philosophical quandaries   ___Riddles

Which of the following interests you most?
___American food   ___Chinese food
___Italian food   ___Mexican food

Which of the following interests you most?
___Blue eyes   ___Brown eyes
___Green eyes   ___Hazel eyes

Which of the following interests you most?
___Middle Earth   ___Neverland
___Oz   ___Wonderland

Which of the following interests you most?
___Free gift with purchase   ___Free shipping
___Half off   ___Tax free

Which of the following interests you most?
___Earthquakes   ___Hurricanes
___Tornados   ___Volcanos

Which of the following interests you most?
___Ballroom dancing   ___Country & Western dancing
___Hip-Hop dancing   ___Swing dancing

Which of the following interests you most?
___Easter Day   ___Independence Day
___St. Patrick's Day   ___Valentine's Day

Which of the following interests you most?
___Watching baseball   ___Watching basketball
___Watching football   ___Watching hockey

RECOMMENDED: *The Secret Me: A Questionnaire Journal*

Multiple Choice

Which of the following interests you most?
___Action films ___Comedy films
___Horror films ___Romantic films

Which of the following interests you most?
___History ___Language arts
___Math ___Science

Which of the following interests you most?
___Eating ___Having sex
___Sleeping ___Socializing

Which of the following interests you most?
___Geothermal energy ___Hydroelectric energy
___Solar energy ___Wind energy

Which of the following interests you most?
___Elementary school ___High school
___Middle school ___Preschool

Which of the following interests you most?
___Chimichangas ___Enchiladas
___Quesadillas ___Tamales

Which of the following interests you most?
___Architecture photography ___Nature photography
___Nude photography ___Space photography

Which of the following interests you most?
___Blonde hair ___Brown hair
___Gray hair ___Red hair

Which of the following interests you most?
___Books ___Comics
___Magazines ___Newspapers

RECOMMENDED: *The Secret Me: A Questionnaire Journal*

What are your thoughts on...

alternative medicine?

_____

_____

_____

_____

_____

_____

survival training?

_____

_____

_____

_____

_____

_____

towing companies?

_____

_____

_____

_____

_____

_____

RECOMMENDED: _The Secret Me: A Biased Perspective_

What are your thoughts on...

convenience fees?

_____

_____

_____

_____

_____

_____

_____

assisted suicide?

_____

_____

_____

_____

_____

_____

black history month?

_____

_____

_____

_____

_____

_____

_____

RECOMMENDED: _The Secret Me: A Biased Perspective_

Would You Do It To Save A Loved One's Life?

Let a bee sting you every day of your life?
[   ]yes [   ]no

Drink disease-free human blood?
[   ]yes [   ]no

Allow scientists to clone you?
[   ]yes [   ]no

Let someone cut one of your feet off?
[   ]yes [   ]no

Lose the ability to speak indefinitely?
[   ]yes [   ]no

Spend a year in complete darkness and solitude?
[   ]yes [   ]no

Purposely gain 500 pounds?
[   ]yes [   ]no

Tattoo Hitler's name on your forehead?
[   ]yes [   ]no

Destroy the pyramids of Giza?
[   ]yes [   ]no

Spend a week alone in a room full of dead bodies?
[   ]yes [   ]no

Be confined to a third world country
for the next ten years of your life?
[   ]yes [   ]no

Pee on a stranger every day of your life?
[   ]yes [   ]no

Lose your ability to orgasm indefinitely?
[   ]yes [   ]no

Let someone cut one of your hands off?
[   ]yes [   ]no

Walk naked through a mile of dirty diapers piled up to your neck?
[   ]yes [   ]no

Dig someone out of their grave, remove all
of their clothes, and rebury them?
[   ]yes [   ]no

RECOMMENDED: *The Secret Me: A Questionnaire Journal*

Would You Do It To Save A Loved One's Life?

Be put to death 25 years from today's date?

[   ]yes [   ]no

Let someone brand twenty random symbols onto your back?

[   ]yes [   ]no

Never again be allowed more than six hours of sleep
in a 24 hour period?

[   ]yes [   ]no

Spend half an hour in a tank containing a live giant squid?

[   ]yes [   ]no

Let someone paralyze you from the waist down?

[   ]yes [   ]no

Bleed from your mouth, nose, eyes and ears for ten minutes
daily for the rest of your life?

[   ]yes [   ]no

Have to live with a lion's tail surgically implanted
directly above your rear?

[   ]yes [   ]no

Let someone drown you and successfully bring you back to life?

[   ]yes [   ]no

Never be able to have or adopt children?

[   ]yes [   ]no

Lose all memory of your life prior to this moment?

[   ]yes [   ]no

Swallow 1000 quarters in a 24 hour period?

[   ]yes [   ]no

Let someone shoot you ten times in places
which wouldn't kill or disable you?

[   ]yes [   ]no

Never again be allowed to consume
more than 1000 calories per day?

[   ]yes [   ]no

Eat a live frog?

[   ]yes [   ]no

RECOMMENDED: *The Secret Me: A Questionnaire Journal*

Your Lists

Memorable things about your birth decade:

1.)_____

2.)_____

3.)_____

4.)_____

5.)_____

6.)_____

7.)_____

8.)_____

9.)_____

10.)_____

Memorable things about the current decade:

1.)_____

2.)_____

3.)_____

4.)_____

5.)_____

6.)_____

7.)_____

8.)_____

9.)_____

10.)_____

RECOMMENDED: *The Secret Me: A List Lover's Keepsake*

Your Lists

Things you looked forward to doing as an adult:

1.)_____
2.)_____
3.)_____
4.)_____
5.)_____
6.)_____
7.)_____
8.)_____
9.)_____
10.)_____

Things which hold you back:

1.)_____
2.)_____
3.)_____
4.)_____
5.)_____
6.)_____
7.)_____
8.)_____
9.)_____
10.)_____

RECOMMENDED: *The Secret Me: A List Lover's Keepsake*

Your Favorite

Author:

_____

Coin:

_____

College:

_____

Color combination:

_____

Fish:

_____

Gaming console:

_____

Kind of cookie:

_____

Mammal:

_____

Meal of the day:

_____

Place to be alone:

_____

President:

_____

Reptile:

_____

Road in your hometown:

_____

Taste:

_____

Temperature:

_____

Thing to dream about:

_____

World country:

_____

RECOMMENDED: _The Secret Me: A Questionnaire Journal_

Your Least Favorite

Author:

Coin:

College:

Color combination:

Fish:

Gaming console:

Kind of cookie:

Mammal:

Meal of the day:

Place to be alone:

President:

Reptile:

Road in your hometown:

Taste:

Temperature:

Thing to dream about:

World country:

RECOMMENDED: *The Secret Me: A Questionnaire Journal*

Music Favorites

ARTIST NAME: _____

ALBUM: _____

LYRIC: _____

Who or what does this artist remind you of?

_____

ARTIST NAME: _____

ALBUM: _____

LYRIC: _____

Who or what does this artist remind you of?

_____

ARTIST NAME: _____

ALBUM: _____

LYRIC: _____

Who or what does this artist remind you of?

_____

ARTIST NAME: _____

ALBUM: _____

LYRIC: _____

Who or what does this artist remind you of?

_____

ARTIST NAME: _____

ALBUM: _____

LYRIC: _____

Who or what does this artist remind you of?

_____

RECOMMENDED: *The Secret Me: A Music Enthusiast's Diary (the unguided edition)*

Music Favorites

ARTIST NAME: _____

ALBUM: _____

LYRIC: _____

Who or what does this artist remind you of?

_____

ARTIST NAME: _____

ALBUM: _____

LYRIC: _____

Who or what does this artist remind you of?

_____

ARTIST NAME: _____

ALBUM: _____

LYRIC: _____

Who or what does this artist remind you of?

_____

ARTIST NAME: _____

ALBUM: _____

LYRIC: _____

Who or what does this artist remind you of?

_____

ARTIST NAME: _____

ALBUM: _____

LYRIC: _____

Who or what does this artist remind you of?

_____

RECOMMENDED: *The Secret Me: A Music Enthusiast's Diary (volume one)*

Music Favorites

ARTIST NAME: _____

ALBUM: _____

LYRIC: _____

Who or what does this artist remind you of?

_____

ARTIST NAME: _____

ALBUM: _____

LYRIC: _____

Who or what does this artist remind you of?

_____

ARTIST NAME: _____

ALBUM: _____

LYRIC: _____

Who or what does this artist remind you of?

_____

ARTIST NAME: _____

ALBUM: _____

LYRIC: _____

Who or what does this artist remind you of?

_____

ARTIST NAME: _____

ALBUM: _____

LYRIC: _____

Who or what does this artist remind you of?

_____

RECOMMENDED: *The Secret Me: A Music Enthusiast's Diary (volume two)*

Music Favorites

ARTIST NAME: _____

ALBUM: _____

LYRIC: _____

Who or what does this artist remind you of?

_____

ARTIST NAME: _____

ALBUM: _____

LYRIC: _____

Who or what does this artist remind you of?

_____

ARTIST NAME: _____

ALBUM: _____

LYRIC: _____

Who or what does this artist remind you of?

_____

ARTIST NAME: _____

ALBUM: _____

LYRIC: _____

Who or what does this artist remind you of?

_____

ARTIST NAME: _____

ALBUM: _____

LYRIC: _____

Who or what does this artist remind you of?

_____

RECOMMENDED: *The Secret Me: A Music Enthusiast's Diary (the unguided edition)*

When Someone Says, You Think...

Adventure

_____

Annoying

_____

Bandages

_____

Barbwire

_____

Beards

_____

Bitter

_____

Boredom

_____

Bottles

_____

Bracelets

_____

Bricks

_____

Change

_____

Coats

_____

Corsets

_____

Coupons   .

_____

Dancing

_____

RECOMMENDED: _The Secret Me: A Questionnaire Journal_

When Someone Says, You Think...

Danger

_____

Delivery

_____

Diamonds

_____

Disgust

_____

Drama

_____

Earthy

_____

Exotic

_____

Faith

_____

Fantasy

_____

Fun

_____

Hairspray

_____

Home

_____

Justice

_____

Karate

_____

Kids

_____

Your Lists

Ways your life differs from your parents' lives:

1.)_____
2.)_____
3.)_____
4.)_____
5.)_____
6.)_____
7.)_____
8.)_____
9.)_____
10.)_____

Things you wish were true:

1.)_____
2.)_____
3.)_____
4.)_____
5.)_____
6.)_____
7.)_____
8.)_____
9.)_____
10.)_____

RECOMMENDED: *The Secret Me: A List Lover's Keepsake*

Your Lists

People you know that might become famous:

1.)_____
2.)_____
3.)_____
4.)_____
5.)_____
6.)_____
7.)_____
8.)_____
9.)_____
10.)_____

People who would do well in The Hunger Games:

1.)_____
2.)_____
3.)_____
4.)_____
5.)_____
6.)_____
7.)_____
8.)_____
9.)_____
10.)_____

RECOMMENDED: *The Secret Me: A List Lover's Keepsake*

Ask Someone

The name of the person you're asking:

_____

In what part of the world do you imagine me being the happiest?

_____

What would you use to lure me into a trap?

_____

What could you see me investing money in?

_____

In a perfect world, who would I end up marrying?

_____

What is your favorite moment we've shared?

_____

What name do you think suits me better than my own?

_____

How many children do you think I was meant to have?

_____

What do you hope I will always remember about you?

_____

What should I try before I die?

_____

Who, not counting me, would you ask these questions of?

_____

RECOMMENDED: *The Secret Me: A Shared Life Log (volume one)*

Ask Someone

The name of the person you're asking:

_____

In what part of the world do you imagine me being the happiest?

_____

What would you use to lure me into a trap?

_____

What could you see me investing money in?

_____

In a perfect world, who would I end up marrying?

_____

What is your favorite moment we've shared?

_____

What name do you think suits me better than my own?

_____

How many children do you think I was meant to have?

_____

What do you hope I will always remember about you?

_____

What should I try before I die?

_____

Who, not counting me, would you ask these questions of?

_____

RECOMMENDED: *The Secret Me: A Shared Life Log (volume two)*

Your Lists

Dares you'd offer while playing Truth or Dare:

1.)_____
2.)_____
3.)_____
4.)_____
5.)_____
6.)_____
7.)_____
8.)_____
9.)_____
10.)_____

Memorable things friends and family have said:

1.)_____
2.)_____
3.)_____
4.)_____
5.)_____
6.)_____
7.)_____
8.)_____
9.)_____
10.)_____

RECOMMENDED: *The Secret Me: A List Lover's Keepsake*

Your Lists

Things you'd want to do in a talent show:

1.)_____
2.)_____
3.)_____
4.)_____
5.)_____
6.)_____
7.)_____
8.)_____
9.)_____
10.)_____

Things you love which others seem to hate:

1.)_____
2.)_____
3.)_____
4.)_____
5.)_____
6.)_____
7.)_____
8.)_____
9.)_____
10.)_____

RECOMMENDED: *The Secret Me: A List Lover's Keepsake*

THIS or THAT

Gray hair	___OR___	Wrinkles
Canada	___OR___	Mexico
Tomato sauce	___OR___	Alfredo sauce
Short stories	___OR___	Long novels
A huge yard	___OR___	No yard
Beer	___OR___	Wine
No science	___OR___	No religion
Brush	___OR___	Floss
Table	___OR___	Booth
Unicorns	___OR___	Dragons
Smooth PB	___OR___	Chunky PB
Crossword puzzles	___OR___	Sudoku puzzles
Boat	___OR___	Plane
Host a party	___OR___	Attend a party
A twin brother	___OR___	A twin sister
Foosball	___OR___	Air hockey
Pets	___OR___	Plants
Asking questions	___OR___	Answering questions
Lakes	___OR___	Rivers
Whole milk	___OR___	Skim milk
Staying up late	___OR___	Sleeping in
Two life partners	___OR___	No life partners
Lectures	___OR___	Debates
Magic show	___OR___	Stand-up comedy
Pants	___OR___	Shorts
Quality	___OR___	Quantity
Be rich	___OR___	Be famous
East coast	___OR___	West coast
Eating too much	___OR___	Eating too little
Work in a team	___OR___	Work alone
Vegan diet	___OR___	Low-carb diet
Ballet	___OR___	Opera

RECOMMENDED: *The Secret Me: A Questionnaire Journal*

THIS or THAT

Socialism	___OR___	Capitalism
Buttons	___OR___	Zippers
Chess	___OR___	Checkers
Poetry	___OR___	Prose
Diamonds	___OR___	Pearls
Puzzles	___OR___	Riddles
Own land	___OR___	Own a home
Ketchup	___OR___	Mustard
Freud	___OR___	Jung
Bar soap	___OR___	Shower gel
Aliens	___OR___	Dinosaurs
Bubble wrap	___OR___	Packing peanuts
Debit	___OR___	Credit
PC	___OR___	Mac
North pole	___OR___	South pole
Tap water	___OR___	Bottled water
Whistling	___OR___	Humming
Turkey	___OR___	Ham
Bright lights	___OR___	Soft lights
Prisons	___OR___	Asylums
Make great money	___OR___	Be your own boss
One story home	___OR___	Two story home
Undecorated walls	___OR___	Overly busy walls
Slides	___OR___	Swings
The 1-5 scale	___OR___	The 1-10 scale
Mental math	___OR___	Spelling
Regular crust pizza	___OR___	Thin crust pizza
Electric razor	___OR___	Disposable razor
Blinds	___OR___	Curtains
Phone calls	___OR___	Text messages
Shaken	___OR___	Stirred
Beef	___OR___	Chicken

RECOMMENDED: *The Secret Me: A Questionnaire Journal*

What are your thoughts on…

promiscuity?

_____

_____

_____

_____

_____

_____

_____

airline security?

_____

_____

_____

_____

_____

the job market?

_____

_____

_____

_____

_____

_____

RECOMMENDED: _The Secret Me: A Biased Perspective_

What are your thoughts on…

music sampling?

_____

_____

_____

_____

_____

_____

electronic voice phenomenon?

_____

_____

_____

_____

_____

_____

shaving?

_____

_____

_____

_____

_____

_____

RECOMMENDED: _The Secret Me: A Biased Perspective_

What are your thoughts on...

tap water?

_____

_____

_____

_____

_____

_____

_____

cheerleading?

_____

_____

_____

_____

_____

for-profit prisons?

_____

_____

_____

_____

_____

_____

RECOMMENDED: _The Secret Me: A Biased Perspective_

What are your thoughts on…

physical education?

_____
_____
_____
_____
_____
_____
_____

Atlantis?

_____
_____
_____
_____
_____
_____

ROTC?

_____
_____
_____
_____
_____
_____

Which of your loved ones is most likely to...

rekindle an old flame?
NAME:_____

complain that something is unfair?
NAME:_____

join a support group?
NAME:_____

take the long way home?
NAME:_____

challenge the accepted historical record?
NAME:_____

pay for something with a check?
NAME:_____

be told they're inappropriate?
NAME:_____

best handle criticism?
NAME:_____

seek out hidden messages in movies and music?
NAME:_____

plead the fifth?
NAME:_____

RECOMMENDED: *The Secret Me: A Companion's Relic (the naming edition)*

Which of your loved ones is most likely to…

become a homicide investigator?

NAME:_____

mute radio or television commercials?

NAME:_____

have trouble admitting when they're wrong?

NAME:_____

take out a high interest loan?

NAME:_____

think themselves misunderstood?

NAME:_____

stay in an abusive relationship?

NAME:_____

dream up their own holiday?

NAME:_____

contract a sexually transmitted disease?

NAME:_____

appreciate a small gift, given at random?

NAME:_____

be considered a socialist?

NAME:_____

RECOMMENDED: *The Secret Me: A Companion's Relic*

Your Lists

Things you weren't taught in grade school:
1.)_____
2.)_____
3.)_____
4.)_____
5.)_____
6.)_____
7.)_____
8.)_____
9.)_____
10.)_____

People you'd like to know better:
1.)_____
2.)_____
3.)_____
4.)_____
5.)_____
6.)_____
7.)_____
8.)_____
9.)_____
10.)_____

RECOMMENDED: *The Secret Me: A List Lover's Keepsake*

Your Lists

Songs whose lyrics you once misunderstood:

1.) _____
2.) _____
3.) _____
4.) _____
5.) _____
6.) _____
7.) _____
8.) _____
9.) _____
10.) _____

Things you'd never do:

1.) _____
2.) _____
3.) _____
4.) _____
5.) _____
6.) _____
7.) _____
8.) _____
9.) _____
10.) _____

RECOMMENDED: *The Secret Me: A List Lover's Keepsake*

Ask Someone

The name of the person you're asking:

_____

In what part of the world do you imagine me being the happiest?

_____

What would you use to lure me into a trap?

_____

What could you see me investing money in?

_____

In a perfect world, who would I end up marrying?

_____

What is your favorite moment we've shared?

_____

What name do you think suits me better than my own?

_____

How many children do you think I was meant to have?

_____

What do you hope I will always remember about you?

_____

What should I try before I die?

_____

Who, not counting me, would you ask these questions of?

_____

RECOMMENDED: _The Secret Me: A Shared Life Log (volume two)_

Ask Someone

The name of the person you're asking:

_____

In what part of the world do you imagine me being the happiest?

_____

What would you use to lure me into a trap?

_____

What could you see me investing money in?

_____

In a perfect world, who would I end up marrying?

_____

What is your favorite moment we've shared?

_____

What name do you think suits me better than my own?

_____

How many children do you think I was meant to have?

_____

What do you hope I will always remember about you?

_____

What should I try before I die?

_____

Who, not counting me, would you ask these questions of?

_____

RECOMMENDED: *The Secret Me: A Shared Life Log (volume one)*

Your Lists

Things which make you feel at ease:

1.)_____

2.)_____

3.)_____

4.)_____

5.)_____

6.)_____

7.)_____

8.)_____

9.)_____

10.)_____

Strange things about yourself:

1.)_____

2.)_____

3.)_____

4.)_____

5.)_____

6.)_____

7.)_____

8.)_____

9.)_____

10.)_____

RECOMMENDED: *The Secret Me: A List Lover's Keepsake*

Your Lists

Things which make great gifts:

1.)_____
2.)_____
3.)_____
4.)_____
5.)_____
6.)_____
7.)_____
8.)_____
9.)_____
10.)_____

Things on your wish list:

1.)_____
2.)_____
3.)_____
4.)_____
5.)_____
6.)_____
7.)_____
8.)_____
9.)_____
10.)_____

RECOMMENDED: *The Secret Me: A List Lover's Keepsake*

On a Scale of 1-10

How important is confidence to you in a life partner?

    1   2   3   4   5   6   7   8   9   10

How important is punctuality to you in a life partner?

    1   2   3   4   5   6   7   8   9   10

How important is a sense of humor to you in a life partner?

    1   2   3   4   5   6   7   8   9   10

How important is creativity to you in a life partner?

    1   2   3   4   5   6   7   8   9   10

How important is orderliness to you in a life partner?

    1   2   3   4   5   6   7   8   9   10

How important is loyalty to you in a life partner?

    1   2   3   4   5   6   7   8   9   10

How important is kindness to you in a life partner?

    1   2   3   4   5   6   7   8   9   10

How important is frugality to you in a life partner?

    1   2   3   4   5   6   7   8   9   10

How important is physical beauty to you in a life partner?

    1   2   3   4   5   6   7   8   9   10

How important is spontaneity to you in a life partner?

    1   2   3   4   5   6   7   8   9   10

RECOMMENDED: *The Secret Me: A Rated Survey*

On a Scale of 1-10

How important is tolerance to you in a life partner?

1   2   3   4   5   6   7   8   9   10

How important is sobriety to you in a life partner?

1   2   3   4   5   6   7   8   9   10

How important is playfulness to you in a life partner?

1   2   3   4   5   6   7   8   9   10

How important is ambition to you in a life partner?

1   2   3   4   5   6   7   8   9   10

How important is wealth to you in a life partner?

1   2   3   4   5   6   7   8   9   10

How important is cleanliness to you in a life partner?

1   2   3   4   5   6   7   8   9   10

How important is talent to you in a life partner?

1   2   3   4   5   6   7   8   9   10

How important is honesty to you in a life partner?

1   2   3   4   5   6   7   8   9   10

How important is generosity to you in a life partner?

1   2   3   4   5   6   7   8   9   10

How important is fitness to you in a life partner?

1   2   3   4   5   6   7   8   9   10

RECOMMENDED: *The Secret Me: A Rated Survey*

Television Favorites

SHOW TITLE: _____

EPISODE: _____

SEASON: _____

Who or what does this show remind you of?

_____

SHOW TITLE: _____

EPISODE: _____

SEASON: _____

Who or what does this show remind you of?

_____

SHOW TITLE: _____

EPISODE: _____

SEASON: _____

Who or what does this show remind you of?

_____

SHOW TITLE: _____

EPISODE: _____

SEASON: _____

Who or what does this show remind you of?

_____

SHOW TITLE: _____

EPISODE: _____

SEASON: _____

Who or what does this show remind you of?

_____

RECOMMENDED: *The Secret Me: A Couch Potato's Take (television edition)*

Television Favorites

SHOW TITLE: _____

EPISODE: _____

SEASON: _____

Who or what does this show remind you of?

_____

SHOW TITLE: _____

EPISODE: _____

SEASON: _____

Who or what does this show remind you of?

_____

SHOW TITLE: _____

EPISODE: _____

SEASON: _____

Who or what does this show remind you of?

_____

SHOW TITLE: _____

EPISODE: _____

SEASON: _____

Who or what does this show remind you of?

_____

SHOW TITLE: _____

EPISODE: _____

SEASON: _____

Who or what does this show remind you of?

_____

RECOMMENDED: *The Secret Me: A Couch Potato's Take (television edition)*

Television Favorites

SHOW TITLE: _____

EPISODE: _____

SEASON: _____

Who or what does this show remind you of?

_____

SHOW TITLE: . _____

EPISODE: _____

SEASON: _____

Who or what does this show remind you of?

_____

SHOW TITLE: _____

EPISODE: _____

SEASON: _____

Who or what does this show remind you of?

_____

SHOW TITLE: _____

EPISODE: _____

SEASON: _____

Who or what does this show remind you of?

_____

SHOW TITLE: _____

EPISODE: _____

SEASON: _____

Who or what does this show remind you of?

_____

RECOMMENDED: *The Secret Me: A Couch Potato's Take (television edition)*

Television Favorites

SHOW TITLE: _____

EPISODE: _____

SEASON: _____

Who or what does this show remind you of?

_____

SHOW TITLE: _____

EPISODE: _____

SEASON: _____

Who or what does this show remind you of?

_____

SHOW TITLE: _____

EPISODE: _____

SEASON: _____

Who or what does this show remind you of?

_____

SHOW TITLE: _____

EPISODE: _____

SEASON: _____

Who or what does this show remind you of?

_____

SHOW TITLE: _____

EPISODE: _____

SEASON: _____

Who or what does this show remind you of?

_____

RECOMMENDED: *The Secret Me: A Couch Potato's Take (television edition)*

At Random

Have you had your tonsils removed?
    [   ]yes [   ]no

                                             Do you like to take naps?
                                              [   ]yes [   ]no

Have you ever created an imaginary friend?
    [   ]yes [   ]no

                              Have you fallen in the shower?
                                              [   ]yes [   ]no

Do you like popcorn?
    [   ]yes [   ]no

                    Do you commonly get carsick while traveling?
                                            [   ]yes [   ]no

Have you had your wisdom teeth removed?
    [   ]yes [   ]no

        Do you usually include a greeting card when giving a gift?
                                            [   ]yes [   ]no

Do you depend on your profession for emotional well-being?
    [   ]yes [   ]no

                        Do you believe yawning is contagious?
                                            [   ]yes [   ]no

Have you attended a family reunion?
    [   ]yes [   ]no

                                Have you written a will?
                                            [   ]yes [   ]no

Do you commonly try free samples at supermarkets?
    [   ]yes [   ]no

                        Do you believe that religion is necessary to
                            make humans treat each other decently?
                                            [   ]yes [   ]no

Have you been locked in a trunk?
    [   ]yes [   ]no

                                        Do you own a safe?
                                        [   ]yes [   ]no

RECOMMENDED: *The Secret Me: A Questionnaire Journal*

At Random

What type of gun would you own, if you had to own one?

_____

What is the biggest deciding factor for you when contemplating whether or not someone is worth marrying?

_____

Have you used a level to hang something?
[   ]yes [   ]no

Have you shaved your arm hair off?
[   ]yes [   ]no

How many weddings have you been in?

_____

What is the angriest you've ever been?

_____

If you were to write a song, who would it be about?

_____

Were you ever held back a year in grade school?
[   ]yes [   ]no

Do you tend to take your work home with you?
[   ]yes [   ]no

What was your mother most passionate about?

_____

What was your father most passionate about?

_____

Your Lists

Qualities you hope for in a child:

1.)_____

2.)_____

3.)_____

4.)_____

5.)_____

6.)_____

7.)_____

8.)_____

9.)_____

10.)_____

Elements of your dream wedding:

1.)_____

2.)_____

3.)_____

4.)_____

5.)_____

6.)_____

7.)_____

8.)_____

9.)_____

10.)_____

RECOMMENDED: *The Secret Me: A List Lover's Keepsake*

Your Lists

People you want in your wedding:
1.)_____
2.)_____
3.)_____
4.)_____
5.)_____
6.)_____
7.)_____
8.)_____
9.)_____
10.)_____

Things which remind you of home:
1.)_____
2.)_____
3.)_____
4.)_____
5.)_____
6.)_____
7.)_____
8.)_____
9.)_____
10.)_____

THIS or THAT

Fish	___OR___	Hunt
Be 60 feet tall	___OR___	Be 6 centimeters tall
Horns	___OR___	Strings
Worry	___OR___	Relax
Built for looks	___OR___	Built for functionality
Microwave	___OR___	Oven
Sequels	___OR___	Prequels
Toothache	___OR___	Earache
A baby boy	___OR___	A baby girl
Crayons	___OR___	Markers
Shooting pool	___OR___	Playing catch
Quotes	___OR___	Memes
Pantyhose	___OR___	Fishnet
Freckles	___OR___	Moles
Vacuum	___OR___	Sweep and mop
Sticks	___OR___	Stones
Lead	___OR___	Follow
Atomic warfare	___OR___	Zombies
Grilled foods	___OR___	Fried foods
Clothes in a dresser	___OR___	Clothes on hangers
Past	___OR___	Future
Save money	___OR___	Save time
Boots	___OR___	Tennis shoes
Surfing	___OR___	Skiing
Fleece	___OR___	Flannel
Warm soda	___OR___	Flat soda
Ninja	___OR___	Pirate
Bad breath	___OR___	Body odor
Air dry	___OR___	Towel dry
Funeral homes	___OR___	Cemeteries
Instrumental	___OR___	Acapella
Curly hair	___OR___	Straight hair

RECOMMENDED: *The Secret Me: A Questionnaire Journal*

THIS or THAT

Theme parks	___OR___	Fairs
Cap	___OR___	Toboggan
Gelatin	___OR___	Pudding
Strip clubs	___OR___	Casinos
Grade school	___OR___	College
Queso	___OR___	Salsa
Trick	___OR___	Treat
Nanny	___OR___	Babysitter
Lotion	___OR___	Lip balm
Pepper spray	___OR___	A taser
T-shirts	___OR___	Button-down shirts
Subway trains	___OR___	Taxi cabs
Cup half-empty	___OR___	Cup half-full
Army	___OR___	Navy
Good sport	___OR___	Sore loser
Over the speed limit	___OR___	Below the speed limit
No music	___OR___	No computers
Patient	___OR___	Impatient
Bracelets	___OR___	Necklaces
Well done	___OR___	Rare
Ebooks	___OR___	Physical books
Monkeys	___OR___	Apes
Say yes	___OR___	Say no
White meat	___OR___	Dark meat
Tight clothes	___OR___	Baggy clothes
Flies	___OR___	Mosquitos
Religious	___OR___	Spiritual
Wake up quickly	___OR___	Wake up slowly
Blanket	___OR___	Comforter
Too much makeup	___OR___	No makeup
Lost with a map	___OR___	Lost with a compass
Be waited on	___OR___	Self-serve

RECOMMENDED: *The Secret Me: A Questionnaire Journal*

Your Lists

Things government should spend more money on:

1.)_____
2.)_____
3.)_____
4.)_____
5.)_____
6.)_____
7.)_____
8.)_____
9.)_____
10.)_____

Things government should spend less money on:

1.)_____
2.)_____
3.)_____
4.)_____
5.)_____
6.)_____
7.)_____
8.)_____
9.)_____
10.)_____

RECOMMENDED: *The Secret Me: A List Lover's Keepsake*

Your Lists

Things you believe are terribly addictive:

1.)_____
2.)_____
3.)_____
4.)_____
5.)_____
6.)_____
7.)_____
8.)_____
9.)_____
10.)_____

Things which make you uncomfortable:

1.)_____
2.)_____
3.)_____
4.)_____
5.)_____
6.)_____
7.)_____
8.)_____
9.)_____
10.)_____

RECOMMENDED: *The Secret Me: A List Lover's Keepsake*

When Someone Says, You Think...

Affection

_____

Censorship

_____

Chance

_____

Coffee

_____

Comfort

_____

Courage

_____

Cruelty

_____

Curiosity

_____

Desire

_____

Disappointment

_____

Doubt

_____

Dreams

_____

Embarrassment

_____

False

_____

Font

_____

When Someone Says, You Think…

Funny

_____

God

_____

Gossip

_____

Greed

_____

Guilt

_____

Habit

_____

Helpless

_____

Hope

_____

Impossible

_____

Insecurity

_____

Jealous

_____

Joy

_____

Lust

_____

Moral

_____

Negativity

_____

What are your thoughts on...

dowsing?

_____

_____

_____

_____

_____

_____

the Pledge of Allegiance?

_____

_____

_____

_____

_____

_____

gateway drugs?

_____

_____

_____

_____

_____

_____

RECOMMENDED: _The Secret Me: A Biased Perspective_

What are your thoughts on...

cryogenics?

_____

_____

_____

_____

_____

_____

_____

hitchhikers?

_____

_____

_____

_____

_____

_____

used video game sales?

_____

_____

_____

_____

_____

_____

What are your thoughts on...

the unemployment rate?

_____

_____

_____

_____

_____

_____

_____

critics?

_____

_____

_____

_____

_____

_____

the Boy Scouts?

_____

_____

_____

_____

_____

_____

RECOMMENDED: _The Secret Me: A Biased Perspective_

What are your thoughts on…

equality?

_____

_____

_____

_____

_____

_____

_____

crop circles?

_____

_____

_____

_____

_____

_____

philosophy?

_____

_____

_____

_____

_____

_____

RECOMMENDED: _The Secret Me: A Biased Perspective_

Multiple Choice

Which of the following interests you most?
___Creating anagrams   ___Making words up
___Pronouncing words backwards   ___Rhyming words

Which of the following interests you most?
___Easy difficulty   ___Hard difficulty
___Insane difficulty   ___Medium difficulty

Which of the following interests you most?
___The Atlantic ocean   ___The Arctic ocean
___The Indian ocean   ___The Pacific ocean

Which of the following interests you most?
___Disappearance mysteries   ___Murder mysteries
___Rape mysteries   ___Theft mysteries

Which of the following interests you most?
___Bass   ___Drums
___Guitars   ___Keyboards

Which of the following interests you most?
___The American Revolutionary War   ___The Civil War
___The Vietnam War   ___World War II

Which of the following interests you most?
___A full bed   ___A king bed
___A queen bed   ___A twin bed

Which of the following interests you most?
___Cocaine   ___Ecstasy
___Heroin   ___Speed

Which of the following interests you most?
___Being a parent   ___Being a politician
___Being a preacher   ___Being a professor

RECOMMENDED: *The Secret Me: A Questionnaire Journal*

Multiple Choice

Which of the following interests you most?
___Astronomy   ___Biology
___Geology   ___Physics

Which of the following interests you most?
___DHL Worldwide Express   ___FedEx
___U.S. Postal Service   ___UPS

Which of the following interests you most?
___A fireplace   ___A garden tub
___A massaging chair   ___A surround sound system

Which of the following interests you most?
___Baby showers   ___Family reunions
___Graduations   ___Weddings

Which of the following interests you most?
___Drawings   ___Paintings
___Photographs   ___Sculptures

Which of the following interests you most?
___Aliens   ___Demonic possessions
___Hauntings   ___Monsters

Which of the following interests you most?
___Betting games   ___Card games
___Dice games   ___Domino games

Which of the following interests you most?
___Lighting   ___Sets
___Special effects   ___Sound

Which of the following interests you most?
___Accounting   ___Managing
___Marketing   ___Programming

RECOMMENDED: *The Secret Me: A Questionnaire Journal*

Your Lists

The most attractive people you've known:

1.)_____

2.)_____

3.)_____

4.)_____

5.)_____

6.)_____

7.)_____

8.)_____

9.)_____

10.)_____

Things you'd like to find in vending machines:

1.)_____

2.)_____

3.)_____

4.)_____

5.)_____

6.)_____

7.)_____

8.)_____

9.)_____

10.)_____

RECOMMENDED: *The Secret Me: A List Lover's Keepsake*

The first books you remember reading:

1.)_____
2.)_____
3.)_____
4.)_____
5.)_____
6.)_____
7.)_____
8.)_____
9.)_____
10.)_____

Dishes common to your family meals:

1.)_____
2.)_____
3.)_____
4.)_____
5.)_____
6.)_____
7.)_____
8.)_____
9.)_____
10.)_____

RECOMMENDED: *The Secret Me: A List Lover's Keepsake*

Ask Someone

The name of the person you're asking:

_____

In what part of the world do you imagine me being the happiest?

_____

What would you use to lure me into a trap?

_____

What could you see me investing money in?

_____

In a perfect world, who would I end up marrying?

_____

What is your favorite moment we've shared?

_____

What name do you think suits me better than my own?

_____

How many children do you think I was meant to have?

_____

What do you hope I will always remember about you?

_____

What should I try before I die?

_____

Who, not counting me, would you ask these questions of?

_____

RECOMMENDED: *The Secret Me: A Shared Life Log (volume one)*

Ask Someone

The name of the person you're asking:

_____

In what part of the world do you imagine me being the happiest?

_____

What would you use to lure me into a trap?

_____

What could you see me investing money in?

_____

In a perfect world, who would I end up marrying?

_____

What is your favorite moment we've shared?

_____

What name do you think suits me better than my own?

_____

How many children do you think I was meant to have?

_____

What do you hope I will always remember about you?

_____

What should I try before I die?

_____

Who, not counting me, would you ask these questions of?

_____

RECOMMENDED: _The Secret Me: A Shared Life Log (volume two)_

Names you'd give or have given to pets:

1.)_____
2.)_____
3.)_____
4.)_____
5.)_____
6.)_____
7.)_____
8.)_____
9.)_____
10.)_____

Great songs for a graduation ceremony:

1.)_____
2.)_____
3.)_____
4.)_____
5.)_____
6.)_____
7.)_____
8.)_____
9.)_____
10.)_____

RECOMMENDED: *The Secret Me: A List Lover's Keepsake*

Your Lists

Things you don't respect:

1.)_____
2.)_____
3.)_____
4.)_____
5.)_____
6.)_____
7.)_____
8.)_____
9.)_____
10.)_____

People you know that are likely to be imprisoned:

1.)_____
2.)_____
3.)_____
4.)_____
5.)_____
6.)_____
7.)_____
8.)_____
9.)_____
10.)_____

RECOMMENDED: *The Secret Me: A List Lover's Keepsake*

Multiple Choice

Which of the following interests you most?
___Ribbon pasta   ___Strand pasta
___Stuffed pasta   ___Tubular pasta

Which of the following interests you most?
___Gums   ___Lips
___Teeth   ___Tongue

Which of the following interests you most?
___Dating a Mexican   ___Dating an African
___Dating an Asian   ___Dating an Indian

Which of the following interests you most?
___Direct mail marketing   ___Door to door marketing
___Email marketing   ___Phone call marketing

Which of the following interests you most?
___Film and television   ___Literature
___Music   ___Video games

Which of the following interests you most?
___Diesel   ___Plus
___Premium   ___Unleaded

Which of the following interests you most?
___Badminton   ___Ping pong
___Tennis   ___Volleyball

Which of the following interests you most?
___Genital piercings   ___Naval piercings
___Nipple piercings   ___Tongue piercings

Which of the following interests you most?
___Fishing   ___Gathering
___Hunting   ___Trapping

RECOMMENDED: *The Secret Me: A Questionnaire Journal*

Multiple Choice

Which of the following interests you most?
___Cricket   ___Lacrosse
___Rugby   ___Soccer

Which of the following interests you most?
___Going 35mph   ___Going 45mph
___Going 55mph   ___Going 65mph

Which of the following interests you most?
___Buffets   ___Fast food establishments
___Home cooked meals   ___Restaurants

Which of the following interests you most?
___Jellyfish   ___Manta ray
___Octopus   ___Squid

Which of the following interests you most?
___Egomania   ___Erotomania
___Kleptomania   ___Pyromania

Which of the following interests you most?
___Baguette cut diamonds   ___Princess cut diamonds
___Round cut diamonds   ___Trillion cut diamonds

Which of the following interests you most?
___A hair transplant   ___Enhancement surgery
___Laser hair removal   ___Liposuction

Which of the following interests you most?
___Rum   ___Tequila
___Vodka   ___Whiskey

Which of the following interests you most?
___A crescent moon   ___A full moon
___A half moon   ___No moon

RECOMMENDED: *The Secret Me: A Questionnaire Journal*

What are your thoughts on...

hospice?

_____

_____

_____

_____

_____

_____

_____

paparazzi?

_____

_____

_____

_____

_____

_____

toxin cleanses?

_____

_____

_____

_____

_____

_____

_____

RECOMMENDED: _The Secret Me: A Biased Perspective_

What are your thoughts on...

perpetual motion?

_____

_____

_____

_____

_____

_____

_____

nursing homes?

_____

_____

_____

_____

_____

_____

classified information?

_____

_____

_____

_____

_____

_____

What are your thoughts on...

acupuncture?

_____

_____

_____

_____

_____

_____

socialism?

_____

_____

_____

_____

_____

_____

popularity?

_____

_____

_____

_____

_____

_____

RECOMMENDED: _The Secret Me: A Biased Perspective_

What are your thoughts on...

magnetic therapy?

_____

_____

_____

_____

_____

_____

_____

Valentine's Day?

_____

_____

_____

_____

_____

_____

school uniforms?

_____

_____

_____

_____

_____

_____

RECOMMENDED: _The Secret Me: A Biased Perspective_

When Someone Says, You Think...

Limousine

_____

Makeup

_____

Manicures

_____

Mask

_____

Moles

_____

Needles

_____

Nervous

_____

Niceties

_____

Nightmares

_____

Pointless

_____

Romance

_____

Sale

_____

Seatbelts

_____

Skirt

_____

Sticky

_____

RECOMMENDED: _The Secret Me: A Questionnaire Journal_

When Someone Says, You Think...

Strings

_____

Success

_____

Sugar

_____

Suicide

_____

Sultry

_____

Sweaters

_____

Tans

_____

Tents

_____

Theory

_____

Toys

_____

Unforgivable

_____

Uniforms

_____

Vest

_____

Wigs

_____

Wings

_____

Your Lists

Reasons you've argued with your parents:

1.)_____
2.)_____
3.)_____
4.)_____
5.)_____
6.)_____
7.)_____
8.)_____
9.)_____
10.)_____

Things you forgot after graduating:

1.)_____
2.)_____
3.)_____
4.)_____
5.)_____
6.)_____
7.)_____
8.)_____
9.)_____
10.)_____

RECOMMENDED: *The Secret Me: A List Lover's Keepsake*

Your Lists

Mistakes most couples make:

1.)_____
2.)_____
3.)_____
4.)_____
5.)_____
6.)_____
7.)_____
8.)_____
9.)_____
10.)_____

People unlikely to befriend each other:

1.)_____
2.)_____
3.)_____
4.)_____
5.)_____
6.)_____
7.)_____
8.)_____
9.)_____
10.)_____

RECOMMENDED: *The Secret Me: A List Lover's Keepsake*

THIS or THAT

Silk	___OR___	Leather
Crossed eyes	___OR___	Crooked teeth
Nausea	___OR___	Fever
Hardbacks	___OR___	Paperbacks
Window seat	___OR___	Aisle seat
Grapes	___OR___	Raisins
Bottle	___OR___	Draft
Take risks	___OR___	Play it safe
Painted toenails	___OR___	Painted fingernails
Manual transmission	___OR___	Auto Transmission
Doing dishes	___OR___	Doing laundry
Real names	___OR___	Nicknames
Circuses	___OR___	Rodeos
All you can eat	___OR___	All you can drink
Visit Mars	___OR___	Visit the moon
White gravy	___OR___	Brown gravy
The 1st amendment	___OR___	The 2nd amendment
Sky diving	___OR___	Bungee jumping
Being disfigured	___OR___	Being disabled
Cereal	___OR___	Oatmeal
Drawing	___OR___	Painting
Freshwater fish tank	___OR___	Saltwater fish tank
Talk shows	___OR___	Soap operas
Play for fun	___OR___	Play to win
Electric guitar	___OR___	Acoustic guitar
Public restrooms	___OR___	Porta potties
Hard candy	___OR___	Chocolates
Competing	___OR___	Spectating
Blue jeans	___OR___	Sweatpants
Eternal torture	___OR___	No afterlife
Knock	___OR___	Ring the doorbell
Walking	___OR___	Running

RECOMMENDED: *The Secret Me: A Questionnaire Journal*

THIS or THAT

Watches	___OR___	Rings
Concerts	___OR___	Sporting events
Elevator	___OR___	Stairs
Batting cages	___OR___	Mini golf
Ice cream	___OR___	Cookies
Pillows	___OR___	Sheets
Breast feeding	___OR___	Bottle feeding
Gas grill	___OR___	Charcoal grill
Satanist	___OR___	Atheist
Large parties	___OR___	Small gatherings
Cold drinks	___OR___	Hot drinks
Friends	___OR___	Family
Ghosts	___OR___	Mermaids
Work too much	___OR___	Not work enough
Trains	___OR___	Buses
Sell	___OR___	Pawn
Picked flowers	___OR___	Potted plants
Comic strips	___OR___	Graphic novels
Having no arms	___OR___	Having no legs
Darts	___OR___	Ping pong
Clear weather	___OR___	Cloudy weather
Baked potatoes	___OR___	Mashed potatoes
Adopting kids	___OR___	Having your own kids
Wooden fence	___OR___	Chain-link fence
Be spit on	___OR___	Be slapped
Motorcycle	___OR___	Van
Crushed ice	___OR___	Cubed ice
Psychic abilities	___OR___	Telekinetic abilities
Sugar	___OR___	No calorie sweetener
Ceiling fans	___OR___	Box fans
Live near mountains	___OR___	Live near the ocean
Overachieve	___OR___	Underachieve

RECOMMENDED: *The Secret Me: A Questionnaire Journal*

Your Lists

Theme parties you'd be interested in hosting:

1.)_____
2.)_____
3.)_____
4.)_____
5.)_____
6.)_____
7.)_____
8.)_____
9.)_____
10.)_____

Celebrities who should make music:

1.)_____
2.)_____
3.)_____
4.)_____
5.)_____
6.)_____
7.)_____
8.)_____
9.)_____
10.)_____

RECOMMENDED: *The Secret Me: A List Lover's Keepsake*

Your Lists

Things which make a person successful:

1.)_____
2.)_____
3.)_____
4.)_____
5.)_____
6.)_____
7.)_____
8.)_____
9.)_____
10.)_____

The best parts of your average day:

1.)_____
2.)_____
3.)_____
4.)_____
5.)_____
6.)_____
7.)_____
8.)_____
9.)_____
10.)_____

RECOMMENDED: *The Secret Me: A List Lover's Keepsake*

At Random

How much sleep would you like to average per night?

_____

Where on Earth would you detonate a nuclear warhead?

_____

What is your biggest source of disappointment?

_____

Estimate the number of times you say "I love you" per week:

_____

At what age should sex education be taught?

_____

Your ideal hug would last how long?

_____

Which religion do you believe is the world's most peaceful?

_____

Where do you usually try to park in parking lots?

_____

You might be featured in a freak-show for what?

_____

What was your very first email address?

_____

Which story of a skyscraper would you want to live on?

_____

RECOMMENDED: _The Secret Me: A Questionnaire Journal_

At Random

How do you prefer your coffee?

_____

What part would you most likely play in a band?

_____

How often do you do laundry?

_____

What is your ring size?

_____

What is the lowest annual income amount you'd be happy making?

_____

Your ideal kiss would last how long?

_____

How long does it normally take you to get ready to go out?

_____

Write out a math problem you have trouble solving:

_____

What disease are you most fearful of contracting?

_____

How often do you shave?

_____

Which religion do you believe is the world's most violent?

_____

RECOMMENDED: _The Secret Me: A Questionnaire Journal_

Video Game Favorites

GAME TITLE: _____

CHARACTER: _____

PART: _____

Who or what does this game remind you of?

_____

GAME TITLE: _____

CHARACTER: _____

PART: _____

Who or what does this game remind you of?

_____

GAME TITLE: _____

CHARACTER: _____

PART: _____

Who or what does this game remind you of?

_____

GAME TITLE: _____

CHARACTER: _____

PART: _____

Who or what does this game remind you of?

_____

GAME TITLE: _____

CHARACTER: _____

PART: _____

Who or what does this game remind you of?

_____

RECOMMENDED: *The Secret Me: A Couch Potato's Take (video game edition)*

Video Game Favorites

GAME TITLE: _____

CHARACTER: _____

PART: _____

Who or what does this game remind you of?

_____

GAME TITLE: _____

CHARACTER: _____

PART: _____

Who or what does this game remind you of?

_____

GAME TITLE: _____

CHARACTER: _____

PART: _____

Who or what does this game remind you of?

_____

GAME TITLE: _____

CHARACTER: _____

PART: _____

Who or what does this game remind you of?

_____

GAME TITLE: _____

CHARACTER: _____

PART: _____

Who or what does this game remind you of?

_____

RECOMMENDED: *The Secret Me: A Couch Potato's Take (video game edition)*

Video Game Favorites

GAME TITLE: _____

CHARACTER: _____

PART: _____

Who or what does this game remind you of?

_____

GAME TITLE: _____

CHARACTER: _____

PART: _____

Who or what does this game remind you of?

_____

GAME TITLE: _____

CHARACTER: _____

PART: _____

Who or what does this game remind you of?

_____

GAME TITLE: _____

CHARACTER: _____

PART: _____

Who or what does this game remind you of?

_____

GAME TITLE: _____

CHARACTER: _____

PART: _____

Who or what does this game remind you of?

_____

RECOMMENDED: *The Secret Me: A Couch Potato's Take (video game edition)*

Video Game Favorites

GAME TITLE: _____

CHARACTER: _____

PART: _____

Who or what does this game remind you of?

_____

GAME TITLE: _____

CHARACTER: _____

PART: _____

Who or what does this game remind you of?

_____

GAME TITLE: _____

CHARACTER: _____

PART: _____

Who or what does this game remind you of?

_____

GAME TITLE: _____

CHARACTER: _____

PART: _____

Who or what does this game remind you of?

_____

GAME TITLE: _____

CHARACTER: _____

PART: _____

Who or what does this game remind you of?

_____

RECOMMENDED: *The Secret Me: A Couch Potato's Take (video game edition)*

On a Scale of 1-10

How important is discretion to you in a life partner?

1   2   3   4   5   6   7   8   9   10

How important is a sense of style to you in a life partner?

1   2   3   4   5   6   7   8   9   10

How important is affection to you in a life partner?

1   2   3   4   5   6   7   8   9   10

How important is decisiveness to you in a life partner?

1   2   3   4   5   6   7   8   9   10

How important is a sense of adventure to you in a life partner?

1   2   3   4   5   6   7   8   9   10

How important is flexibility to you in a life partner?

1   2   3   4   5   6   7   8   9   10

How important is availability to you in a life partner?

1   2   3   4   5   6   7   8   9   10

How important is humility to you in a life partner?

1   2   3   4   5   6   7   8   9   10

How important is sexual appetite to you in a life partner?

1   2   3   4   5   6   7   8   9   10

How important is religiosity to you in a life partner?

1   2   3   4   5   6   7   8   9   10

RECOMMENDED: *The Secret Me: A Rated Survey*

On a Scale of 1-10

How important is tact to you in a life partner?

   1   2   3   4   5   6   7   8   9   10

How important is curiosity to you in a life partner?

   1   2   3   4   5   6   7   8   9   10

How important is independence to you in a life partner?

   1   2   3   4   5   6   7   8   9   10

How important is posture to you in a life partner?

   1   2   3   4   5   6   7   8   9   10

How important is cautiousness to you in a life partner?

   1   2   3   4   5   6   7   8   9   10

How important is sensitivity to you in a life partner?

   1   2   3   4   5   6   7   8   9   10

How important is uniqueness to you in a life partner?

   1   2   3   4   5   6   7   8   9   10

How important is courtesy to you in a life partner?

   1   2   3   4   5   6   7   8   9   10

How important is romanticism to you in a life partner?

   1   2   3   4   5   6   7   8   9   10

How important is intelligence to you in a life partner?

   1   2   3   4   5   6   7   8   9   10

RECOMMENDED: *The Secret Me: A Rated Survey*

Your Lists

Women's most basic needs:

1.)_____

2.)_____

3.)_____

4.)_____

5.)_____

6.)_____

7.)_____

8.)_____

9.)_____

10.)_____

Men's most basic needs:

1.)_____

2.)_____

3.)_____

4.)_____

5.)_____

6.)_____

7.)_____

8.)_____

9.)_____

10.)_____

RECOMMENDED: *The Secret Me: A List Lover's Keepsake*

Your Lists

Free things you enjoy doing:

1.)_____
2.)_____
3.)_____
4.)_____
5.)_____
6.)_____
7.)_____
8.)_____
9.)_____
10.)_____

The best dressers you know:

1.)_____
2.)_____
3.)_____
4.)_____
5.)_____
6.)_____
7.)_____
8.)_____
9.)_____
10.)_____

RECOMMENDED: *The Secret Me: A List Lover's Keepsake*

Ask Someone

The name of the person you're asking:

_____

In what part of the world do you imagine me being the happiest?

_____

What would you use to lure me into a trap?

_____

What could you see me investing money in?

_____

In a perfect world, who would I end up marrying?

_____

What is your favorite moment we've shared?

_____

What name do you think suits me better than my own?

_____

How many children do you think I was meant to have?

_____

What do you hope I will always remember about you?

_____

What should I try before I die?

_____

Who, not counting me, would you ask these questions of?

_____

RECOMMENDED: *The Secret Me: A Shared Life Log (volume two)*

Ask Someone

The name of the person you're asking:

_____

In what part of the world do you imagine me being the happiest?

_____

What would you use to lure me into a trap?

_____

What could you see me investing money in?

_____

In a perfect world, who would I end up marrying?

_____

What is your favorite moment we've shared?

_____

What name do you think suits me better than my own?

_____

How many children do you think I was meant to have?

_____

What do you hope I will always remember about you?

_____

What should I try before I die?

_____

Who, not counting me, would you ask these questions of?

_____

RECOMMENDED: _The Secret Me: A Shared Life Log (volume one)_

Your Lists

Memorable movie taglines:

1.)_____

2.)_____

3.)_____

4.)_____

5.)_____

6.)_____

7.)_____

8.)_____

9.)_____

10.)_____

Gifts you'd give if you were suddenly rich:

1.)_____

2.)_____

3.)_____

4.)_____

5.)_____

6.)_____

7.)_____

8.)_____

9.)_____

10.)_____

RECOMMENDED: *The Secret Me: A List Lover's Keepsake*

Your Lists

Air freshener and candle scents you like:

1.)_____
2.)_____
3.)_____
4.)_____
5.)_____
6.)_____
7.)_____
8.)_____
9.)_____
10.)_____

Television channels you like:

1.)_____
2.)_____
3.)_____
4.)_____
5.)_____
6.)_____
7.)_____
8.)_____
9.)_____
10.)_____

Which Would You Prefer?

One lover in a lifetime
___OR___
One hundred lovers in a lifetime

Every human owning a firearm
___OR___
No humans owning firearms

The ability to read others' thoughts
___OR___
The ability to watch others' dreams

Losing all of your belongings
___OR___
Losing the ability to climax

A partner that cries often
___OR___
A partner that never feels sadness

Dying slow and painfully at age 100
___OR___
Dying quick and painlessly at age 50

Children allowed to purchase pornography
___OR___
Children allowed to purchase tobacco

Vastly increased intelligence for our species
___OR___
Saving the lives of a billion starving people

Being rich, doing something you despise for a living
___OR___
Being poor, doing something you enjoy for a living

RECOMMENDED: *The Secret Me: A Questionnaire Journal*

Which Would You Prefer?

The deaths of one billion humans in third world countries
___OR___
The deaths of one hundred million humans in developed nations

A partner who has trouble saving money
___OR___
A partner who swears a lot in mixed company

Reparations for African Americans
___OR___
Immediate citizenship for all illegal aliens

Medicinal testing on any non-human animals permitted
___OR___
The extinction of an endangered species

Being awake for no more than four hours per day
___OR___
The legalization of long and violent death row inmate executions

No trees left on the planet
___OR___
An inability to see stars in the night sky

The legalization of late term abortions
___OR___
Having nightmares every time you sleep

No action taken to reverse the effects of global warming
___OR___
Never being allowed to make more than $40,000 annually

Appearing to be 80 years old throughout your lifetime
___OR___
Appearing to be 8 years old throughout your lifetime

RECOMMENDED: *The Secret Me: A Questionnaire Journal*

What are your thoughts on...

anti-depressants?

_____
_____
_____
_____
_____
_____
_____

infinity?

_____
_____
_____
_____
_____
_____

public transportation?

_____
_____
_____
_____
_____
_____
_____

RECOMMENDED: _The Secret Me: A Biased Perspective_

What are your thoughts on...

faster-than-light travel?

_____

_____

_____

_____

_____

_____

_____

leaf blowers?

_____

_____

_____

_____

_____

_____

the historicity of Jesus?

_____

_____

_____

_____

_____

_____

What are your thoughts on...

food options in public schools?

_____

_____

_____

_____

_____

_____

_____

generic brands?

_____

_____

_____

_____

_____

_____

auto mechanics?

_____

_____

_____

_____

_____

_____

What are your thoughts on…

sleep?

_____
_____
_____
_____
_____
_____
_____

intimacy?

_____
_____
_____
_____
_____
_____

facial hair?

_____
_____
_____
_____
_____
_____
_____

RECOMMENDED: *The Secret Me: A Biased Perspective*

THIS or THAT

Owls	___OR___	Bats
Delivery	___OR___	Takeout
Multiply	___OR___	Divide
Solid deodorant	___OR___	Gel deodorant
FBI	___OR___	CIA
Brick home	___OR___	Log cabin
Cinnamon	___OR___	Mint
Song verses	___OR___	Song choruses
Park ranger	___OR___	Security guard
Lemons	___OR___	Limes
Boxing	___OR___	Wrestling
Highways	___OR___	FM roads
Nose hair	___OR___	Ear hair
Ant farm	___OR___	Sea-Monkey hatchery
Rent	___OR___	Buy
1st person shooters	___OR___	3rd person shooters
Marble	___OR___	Steel
Physical address	___OR___	PO Box
Rice	___OR___	Noodles
Headset	___OR___	Handset
Bees	___OR___	Butterflies
Towel	___OR___	Robe
Odd	___OR___	Even
Philosophy	___OR___	Psychology
Nuts	___OR___	Beef jerky
Being tactful	___OR___	Being blunt
Hills	___OR___	Plains
Yacht	___OR___	RV
Horse races	___OR___	Dog races
Red pepper	___OR___	Parmesan
Match	___OR___	Lighter
Old favorite	___OR___	The next big thing

RECOMMENDED: *The Secret Me: A Questionnaire Journal*

THIS or THAT

Fake plants	___OR___	Real plants
Being heard	___OR___	Being seen
Shampoo	___OR___	Conditioner
A younger partner	___OR___	An older partner
Road trips	___OR___	Cruises
Taco	___OR___	Burrito
Gymnastics	___OR___	Figure skating
Museums	___OR___	Historical landmarks
Olives	___OR___	Cherries
Back seat	___OR___	Front seat
Oil paintings	___OR___	Watercolor paintings
Penguin	___OR___	Ostrich
Fireworks	___OR___	Laser light shows
Constipation	___OR___	Diarrhea
Walk during the day	___OR___	Walk at night
Vehicle with a stereo	___OR___	Vehicle with AC
Garlic	___OR___	Basil
An overweight date	___OR___	An underweight date
Bowling	___OR___	Golfing
Popularity	___OR___	Knowledge
Biscuits	___OR___	Cornbread
Shots	___OR___	Suppositories
A bug zapper	___OR___	Bug repellent spray
Gym workouts	___OR___	Outdoor workouts
Add	___OR___	Subtract
Pills	___OR___	Liquid medications
Convenience	___OR___	Challenge
Sidewalks	___OR___	Trails
A tactical approach	___OR___	A forceful approach
Zero gravity	___OR___	50% gravity
Tinted windows	___OR___	Non-tinted windows
Neon lights	___OR___	Black lights

RECOMMENDED: *The Secret Me: A Questionnaire Journal*

Your Lists

Things you want most in a social website:

1.)_____

2.)_____

3.)_____

4.)_____

5.)_____

6.)_____

7.)_____

8.)_____

9.)_____

10.)_____

Reasons to cut someone out of your life:

1.)_____

2.)_____

3.)_____

4.)_____

5.)_____

6.)_____

7.)_____

8.)_____

9.)_____

10.)_____

RECOMMENDED: *The Secret Me: A List Lover's Keepsake*

Your Lists

People you often think of while listening to music:

1.)_____
2.)_____
3.)_____
4.)_____
5.)_____
6.)_____
7.)_____
8.)_____
9.)_____
10.)_____

Songs you simply cannot sing well:

1.)_____
2.)_____
3.)_____
4.)_____
5.)_____
6.)_____
7.)_____
8.)_____
9.)_____
10.)_____

RECOMMENDED: *The Secret Me: A List Lover's Keepsake*

Ask Someone

The name of the person you're asking:

_____

In what part of the world do you imagine me being the happiest?

_____

What would you use to lure me into a trap?

_____

What could you see me investing money in?

_____

In a perfect world, who would I end up marrying?

_____

What is your favorite moment we've shared?

_____

What name do you think suits me better than my own?

_____

How many children do you think I was meant to have?

_____

What do you hope I will always remember about you?

_____

What should I try before I die?

_____

Who, not counting me, would you ask these questions of?

_____

RECOMMENDED: *The Secret Me: A Shared Life Log (volume one)*

Ask Someone

The name of the person you're asking:

_____

In what part of the world do you imagine me being the happiest?

_____

What would you use to lure me into a trap?

_____

What could you see me investing money in?

_____

In a perfect world, who would I end up marrying?

_____

What is your favorite moment we've shared?

_____

What name do you think suits me better than my own?

_____

How many children do you think I was meant to have?

_____

What do you hope I will always remember about you?

_____

What should I try before I die?

_____

Who, not counting me, would you ask these questions of?

_____

RECOMMENDED: _The Secret Me: A Shared Life Log (volume two)_

Your Lists

Funny things to say while climaxing:

1.)_____
2.)_____
3.)_____
4.)_____
5.)_____
6.)_____
7.)_____
8.)_____
9.)_____
10.)_____

Movies you've seen more than once in theaters:

1.)_____
2.)_____
3.)_____
4.)_____
5.)_____
6.)_____
7.)_____
8.)_____
9.)_____
10.)_____

RECOMMENDED: *The Secret Me: A List Lover's Keepsake*

Your Lists

Resolutions for the next new year:

1.)_____

2.)_____

3.)_____

4.)_____

5.)_____

6.)_____

7.)_____

8.)_____

9.)_____

10.)_____

Things which make sleep come easier:

1.)_____

2.)_____

3.)_____

4.)_____

5.)_____

6.)_____

7.)_____

8.)_____

9.)_____

10.)_____

RECOMMENDED: *The Secret Me: A List Lover's Keepsake*

When Someone Says, You Think...

Neglect

_____

Obsession

_____

Offend

_____

Pain

_____

Panic

_____

Passion

_____

Perfection

_____

Pity

_____

Polite

_____

Positivity

_____

Pride

_____

Propaganda

_____

Regret

_____

Relief

_____

Religion

_____

When Someone Says, You Think...

Satisfaction

_____

Serenity

_____

Sexy

_____

Shock

_____

Sorrow

_____

Stress

_____

Taboo

_____

Tease

_____

Time

_____

Torture

_____

Triumph

_____

Trust

_____

Truth

_____

Work

_____

Youth

_____

RECOMMENDED: _The Secret Me: A Questionnaire Journal_

Film Favorites

FILM TITLE: _____

CHARACTER: _____

LINE: _____

Who or what does this film remind you of?

_____

FILM TITLE: _____

CHARACTER: _____

LINE: _____

Who or what does this film remind you of?

_____

FILM TITLE: _____

CHARACTER: _____

LINE: _____

Who or what does this film remind you of?

_____

FILM TITLE: _____

CHARACTER: _____

LINE: _____

Who or what does this film remind you of?

_____

FILM TITLE: _____

CHARACTER: _____

LINE: _____

Who or what does this film remind you of?

_____

RECOMMENDED: *The Secret Me: A Film Fanatic's Record*

Film Favorites

FILM TITLE: _____

CHARACTER: _____

LINE: _____

Who or what does this film remind you of?

_____

FILM TITLE: _____

CHARACTER: _____

LINE: _____

Who or what does this film remind you of?

_____

FILM TITLE: _____

CHARACTER: _____

LINE: _____

Who or what does this film remind you of?

_____

FILM TITLE: _____

CHARACTER: _____

LINE: _____

Who or what does this film remind you of?

_____

FILM TITLE: _____

CHARACTER: _____

LINE: _____

Who or what does this film remind you of?

_____

RECOMMENDED: *The Secret Me: A Film Fanatic's Record*

Film Favorites

FILM TITLE: _____

CHARACTER: _____

LINE: _____

Who or what does this film remind you of?

_____

FILM TITLE: _____

CHARACTER: _____

LINE: _____

Who or what does this film remind you of?

_____

FILM TITLE: _____

CHARACTER: _____

LINE: _____

Who or what does this film remind you of?

_____

FILM TITLE: _____

CHARACTER: _____

LINE: _____

Who or what does this film remind you of?

_____

FILM TITLE: _____

CHARACTER: _____

LINE: _____

Who or what does this film remind you of?

_____

RECOMMENDED: *The Secret Me: A Film Fanatic's Record*

Film Favorites

FILM TITLE: _____

CHARACTER: _____

LINE: _____

Who or what does this film remind you of?

_____

FILM TITLE: _____

CHARACTER: _____

LINE: _____

Who or what does this film remind you of?

_____

FILM TITLE: _____

CHARACTER: _____

LINE: _____

Who or what does this film remind you of?

_____

FILM TITLE: _____

CHARACTER: _____

LINE: _____

Who or what does this film remind you of?

_____

FILM TITLE: _____

CHARACTER: _____

LINE: _____

Who or what does this film remind you of?

_____

RECOMMENDED: *The Secret Me: A Film Fanatic's Record*

Your Favorite

Book for young people:

_____

Color to wear:

_____

First Lady:

_____

Grade in school:

_____

Kind of cake:

_____

Kind of pie:

_____

Place on your body to spray perfume or cologne:

_____

Pool depth:

_____

Shape:

_____

Soup:

_____

Teacher:

_____

Thing to shop for:

_____

Thing to talk about:

_____

Time of day to exercise:

_____

Type of chip:

_____

Vice President:

_____

Word:

_____

RECOMMENDED: *The Secret Me: A Questionnaire Journal*

Your Least Favorite

Book for young people:

_____

Color to wear:

_____

First Lady:

_____

Grade in school:

_____

Kind of cake:

_____

Kind of pie:

_____

Place on your body to spray perfume or cologne:

_____

Pool depth:

_____

Shape:

_____

Soup:

_____

Teacher:

_____

Thing to shop for:

_____

Thing to talk about:

_____

Time of day to exercise:

_____

Type of chip:

_____

Vice President:

_____

Word:

_____

RECOMMENDED: *The Secret Me: A Questionnaire Journal*

Your Lists

Elements of your dream home:

1.)_____
2.)_____
3.)_____
4.)_____
5.)_____
6.)_____
7.)_____
8.)_____
9.)_____
10.)_____

People you believe would haunt you if they could:

1.)_____
2.)_____
3.)_____
4.)_____
5.)_____
6.)_____
7.)_____
8.)_____
9.)_____
10.)_____

RECOMMENDED: *The Secret Me: A List Lover's Keepsake*

Your Lists

Hurtful things others have said to you:

1.)_____

2.)_____

3.)_____

4.)_____

5.)_____

6.)_____

7.)_____

8.)_____

9.)_____

10.)_____

Artists which you believe are wrongly ridiculed:

1.)_____

2.)_____

3.)_____

4.)_____

5.)_____

6.)_____

7.)_____

8.)_____

9.)_____

10.)_____

Would You Do It To Save A Stranger's Life?

Let a bee sting you every day of your life?
[   ]yes [   ]no

Drink disease-free human blood?
[   ]yes [   ]no

Allow scientists to clone you?
[   ]yes [   ]no

Let someone cut one of your feet off?
[   ]yes [   ]no

Lose the ability to speak indefinitely?
[   ]yes [   ]no

Spend a year in complete darkness and solitude?
[   ]yes [   ]no

Purposely gain 500 pounds?
[   ]yes [   ]no

Tattoo Hitler's name on your forehead?
[   ]yes [   ]no

Destroy the pyramids of Giza?
[   ]yes [   ]no

Spend a week alone in a room full of dead bodies?
[   ]yes [   ]no

Be confined to a third world country
for the next ten years of your life?
[   ]yes [   ]no

Pee on a stranger every day of your life?
[   ]yes [   ]no

Lose your ability to orgasm indefinitely?
[   ]yes [   ]no

Let someone cut one of your hands off?
[   ]yes [   ]no

Walk naked through a mile of dirty diapers piled up to your neck?
[   ]yes [   ]no

Dig someone out of their grave, remove all
of their clothes, and rebury them?
[   ]yes [   ]no

RECOMMENDED: *The Secret Me: A Questionnaire Journal*

Would You Do It To Save A Stranger's Life?

Be put to death 25 years from today's date?

[   ]yes [   ]no

Let someone brand twenty random symbols onto your back?

[   ]yes [   ]no

Never again be allowed more than six hours of sleep
in a 24 hour period?

[   ]yes [   ]no

Spend half an hour in a tank containing a live giant squid?

[   ]yes [   ]no

Let someone paralyze you from the waist down?

[   ]yes [   ]no

Bleed from your mouth, nose, eyes and ears for ten minutes
daily for the rest of your life?

[   ]yes [   ]no

Have to live with a lion's tail surgically implanted
directly above your rear?

[   ]yes [   ]no

Let someone drown you and successfully bring you back to life?

[   ]yes [   ]no

Never be able to have or adopt children?

[   ]yes [   ]no

Lose all memory of your life prior to this moment?

[   ]yes [   ]no

Swallow 1000 quarters in a 24 hour period?

[   ]yes [   ]no

Let someone shoot you ten times in places
which wouldn't kill or disable you?

[   ]yes [   ]no

Never again be allowed to consume
more than 1000 calories per day?

[   ]yes [   ]no

Eat a live frog?

[   ]yes [   ]no

RECOMMENDED: *The Secret Me: A Questionnaire Journal*

What are your thoughts on...

preservatives?

_____

_____

_____

_____

_____

_____

_____

lie detector tests?

_____

_____

_____

_____

_____

_____

sex appeal?

_____

_____

_____

_____

_____

_____

RECOMMENDED: _The Secret Me: Biased Perspective_

What are your thoughts on...

parties?

_____

_____

_____

_____

_____

_____

feng shui?

_____

_____

_____

_____

_____

karaoke?

_____

_____

_____

_____

_____

_____

Multiple Choice

Which of the following interests you most?
___Afternoons   ___Evenings
___Mornings   ___Nights

Which of the following interests you most?
___A backyard fire pit   ___A rooftop patio
___A theater room   ___An indoor pool

Which of the following interests you most?
___Crab   ___Lobster
___Oysters   ___Shrimp

Which of the following interests you most?
___A 12 ounce drink   ___A 20 ounce drink
___A 32 ounce drink   ___A 40 ounce drink

Which of the following interests you most?
___Dimes   ___Nickels
___Pennies   ___Quarters

Which of the following interests you most?
___Eye shadow   ___Foundation
___Lipstick   ___Mascara

Which of the following interests you most?
___A back massage   ___A foot massage
___A hand massage   ___A neck massage

Which of the following interests you most?
___Beauty magazines   ___Celebrity magazines
___Gaming magazines   ___Science magazines

Which of the following interests you most?
___A 1 hour movie   ___A 1 ½ hour movie
___A 2 hour movie   ___A 3 hour movie

RECOMMENDED: *The Secret Me: A Questionnaire Journal*

Multiple Choice

Which of the following interests you most?
___Playing baseball   ___Playing basketball
___Playing football   ___Playing hockey

Which of the following interests you most?
___Ear piercings   ___Eyebrow piercings
___Nose piercings   ___Lip piercings

Which of the following interests you most?
___A floating, water-top home   ___A hovering home in the sky
___An underground home   ___An underwater home

Which of the following interests you most?
___Bigfoot   ___Mothman
___The Chupacabra   ___The Loch Ness Monster

Which of the following interests you most?
___1 player games   ___2 player games
___3 player games   ___4 player games

Which of the following interests you most?
___Banking   ___Car sales
___Insurance   ___Real estate

Which of the following interests you most?
___Ghosts   ___Vampires
___Werewolves   ___Zombies

Which of the following interests you most?
___Bicycles   ___Skateboards
___Skates   ___Scooters

Which of the following interests you most?
___Dolphins   ___Manatees
___Sharks   ___Whales

RECOMMENDED: *The Secret Me: A Questionnaire Journal*

Even <u>MORE</u> Before You Die, You'd Like To…

46.) _____

47.) _____

48.) _____

49.) _____

50.) _____

51.) _____

52.) _____

53.) _____

54.) _____

55.) _____

56.) _____

57.) _____

58.) _____

59.) _____

60.) _____

61.) _____

62.) _____

RECOMMENDED: *The Secret Me: A Questionnaire Journal*

Even <u>MORE</u> Before You Die, You'd Like To ...

63.)_____

64.)_____

65.)_____

66.)_____

67.)_____

68.)_____

69.)_____

70.)_____

71.)_____

72.)_____

73.)_____

74.)_____

75.)_____

76.)_____

77.)_____

78.)_____

79.)_____

RECOMMENDED: *The Secret Me: A Questionnaire Journal*

Even **MORE** Before You Die, You'd Like To ...

80.)_____

81.)_____

82.)_____

83.)_____

84.)_____

85.)_____

86.)_____

87.)_____

88.)_____

89.)_____

90.)_____

In the event of your death, you want this journal given to:

_____

Your signature: Date completed:

_____   _____

THE EXPERIENCE DOESN'T END HERE

Complete your collection of The Secret Me books today
by purchasing any of the following online:

The Secret Me: A Biased Perspective

The Secret Me: A Companion's Relic

The Secret Me: A Companion's Relic (naming edition)

The Secret Me: A Couch Potato's Take (table game edition)

The Secret Me: A Couch Potato's Take (television edition)

The Secret Me: A Couch Potato's Take (video game edition)

The Secret Me: A Fantasy Manifesto

The Secret Me: A Film Fanatic's Record

The Secret Me: A Harry Potter Examination

The Secret Me: A List Lover's Keepsake

The Secret Me: A Music Enthusiast's Diary (volume one)

The Secret Me: A Music Enthusiast's Diary (volume two)

The Secret Me: A Music Enthusiast's Diary (unguided edition)

The Secret Me: A Questionnaire Journal

The Secret Me: A Questionnaire Journal 2

The Secret Me: A Questionnaire Journal for Teens

The Secret Me: A Rated Survey

The Secret Me: A Rated Survey 2

The Secret Me: A Shared Life Log (volume one)

The Secret Me: A Shared Life Log (volume two)

Most every book in the series can be obtained online for under $10!
They ship fast, and often free, from the world's
most trusted book source.

Made in the USA
Middletown, DE
01 May 2015